SHADES OF BLUE:
The Decline and Fall of Lady Day

by Steven Carl McCasland

Dearest Celia,
I love you.
Until next time . . .
Love,
Steven

PRODUCTION HISTORY

Shades of Blue: The Decline and Fall of Lady Day premiered at
The Dorothy Strelsin Theatre in 2014, produced by The
Beautiful Soup Theater Collective. The production was directed
by the playwright with Lighting Design by Molly Tiede,
Costume Design by Somie Pak and Stage Managed by Hailli
Ridsdale. The cast was as follows:

BILLIE HOLIDAY: Suzanne Froix
TALLULAH BANKHEAD: Kristen Gehling
JOE GLASER: Orlando Iriarte
LOUIS MCKAY: Ron Denson
LAURA "BIG RED" LIVINGSTONE: Alana Inez
DOROTHY PARKER: Laurie Sammeth
NURSE: Somie Pak
SADIE: Bettina Denson

CHARACTERS

BILLIE HOLIDAY. 40's. African American. A singer.

TALLULAH BANKHEAD. 50's. An actress.

JOE GLASER. 40's. Caucasian. Billie's agent.

LOUIS MCKAY. 40's. African American. Billie's husband.

LAURA "BIG RED" LIVINGSTONE. 30's. Bi-racial. A dancer and one of Billie's many lovers.

NURSE. 50's. White. Actress may double as DOROTHY PARKER.

DOROTHY PARKER. 50's. White. A writer and Tallulah's friend. Actress may double as NURSE.

SADIE FAGAN. 40's or 50's. Billie's mother. A ghostly presence from the past.

TIME AND PLACE

1939-1944. Various locations in Billie Holiday's life. Nightclubs, hospitals, offices, dressing rooms and bedrooms.

AUTHOR'S NOTE

It's less of a play and more of a jazz set. But be careful not to think of the monologues as "turns". This is Billie's story.

The play should flow seamlessly. Yes, there are blackouts, but they are merely used as punctuation. You could cut all or some of them if your lighting designer is smart enough. Scene changes should be instantaneous and the pace should never slow down. Whenever Billie - or anyone, really - uses the telephone, don't assume you need a phone. Their attention and *in*tention will do the work for us.

Scenes and interludes should be lit differently if possible.

The line-breaks don't make it poetry. Think of them as shifts in thought, attack and intention.

A / before a word (i.e /note) means that the next speaker should begin overlapping at that point.

Please refrain from ending with Billie Holiday's legendary recording of "I'll Be Seeing You". You might be tempted to. Don't give in.

SHADES OF BLUE:
The Decline and Fall of Lady Day

Scene 1

(At curtain, TALLULAH BANKHEAD is smoking alone at a table in a dive bar. The invisible audience around her is applauding as an unseen and unheard BILLIE HOLIDAY exits the stage. We should never hear her sing. After the applause dines down, we hear drinks being drunk, conversations being had, chairs being moved around the club. A moment passes as JOE GLASER approaches in a navy blue suit. He isn't very handsome. He isn't very nice. And he certainly isn't very classy.)

JOE.
Caught you staring.
It's okay, Miss B.
Everybody does.
Stare away.
Tell me, is it the legs?
I love a pair of legs.
Or is it that tough hair of Lady Day's?
Louis says it's those chocolate eyes
but Big Red
- that's Lady's oldest pal -
Big Red says it's that long black neck where all those sweet sounds get born like babies.
Joe Glaser, Miss B.
Her right hand yes man.

TALLULAH.
Her agent.

JOE.
Yes, ma'am.

TALLULAH.
Cocksuckers.
All of you.
Tell her I'm here.

JOE.
Lady doesn't like interruptions between sets.

TALLULAH.
She'll like this one.
It's been a long time, Mr.--

JOE.
Glaser.

TALLULAH.
I won't remember that so don't go expecting a miracle.
Tell her Tallulah Bankhead is here tonight.
That she'd like to see her.
Tell her we'll lock the door this time.
(Beat.)
Don't blush, Mr. Glaser.
It isn't very professional.
Go on and tell her.
Tell her Loolie's thirsty.
(Beat. He looks at her for a moment, and then goes.)
And tell the waiter to bring me another drink while I wait.

(Blackout.)

Scene 2

(BILLIE HOLIDAY'S dressing room. The wallpaper is peeling. The room is claustrophobic. The furniture is shabby and filthy. Lady Day is not performing at The Palace. TALLULAH stands in the doorway. BILLIE is on the couch, seated in a cocktail dress. Her legs akimbo. The light from the hallway door is the only one we can see.)

BILLIE.
Well.

TALLULAH.
Well, indeed.

BILLIE.
Close that door.

TALLULAH.
Turn on a light.

BILLIE.
I get enough fuckin' light on stage.
What do I need light now for?
Not everyone's like you, Banky, baby.
Not everyone loves all that
light.

TALLULAH
.Your voice is shot.

BILLIE.
And you look old.
Why you here?

TALLULAH.
All in good time.
What is it?
Look at your arms.
what is it?
Tar?
Smack?
What are you up to?

BILLIE.
None of your goddamn business what I'm up to.
Close the door.

TALLULAH.
When you turn on a fucking light

I will close the fucking door.
I didn't come here to talk in the dark.

(Beat. It's a standoff. But BILLIE gives up too easily. The light is right by the couch. She hits it. It's hideous, hard, but it's what TALLULAH asked for. Just as abruptly and swiftly, she slams the door shut behind her)

TALLULAH.
A book.

BILLIE.
What?

TALLULAH.
Billie Holiday is going to write a book.

BILLIE.
They pay me enough,
sure,
why not?

TALLULAH.
Have you ever read a book?

BILLIE.
I read yours.

TALLULAH.
And?
Couldn't put it down?

BILLIE.
I wasn't even mentioned.

TALLULAH.
Of course, you weren't.
What would I say?
Everything between Billie Holiday's legs tasted like chocolate?

BILLIE.

Not even a little mention.

TALLULAH.
You'd have liked it?

BILLIE.
Of course.

TALLULAH.
Bullshit.
You would've hated it.
You would've rung me up drunk as a skunk and let me have it.

(BILLIE rises and clumsily takes a step or two forward. She wiggles a finger, a hand, an arm at TALLULAH.)

BILLIE.
Aw, come on.
Come on and dance with me, lady.
I like it cheek to cheek.
Come on and dance those legs over to me.

TALLULAH.
Aren't you tired?
Aren't you tired from always bullshitting?

BILLIE.
I saw you in a play last Tuesday.
Or maybe it was a movie.
It was very whiskey out that evening and the theatre was darker than Harlem on a Thursday after midnight so I don't remember which.
Maybe it was a movie because I remember you larger than life or
maybe it was a play because I remember the color of your thighs or
maybe it was neither and I saw your eyes across the room when I was singing.

TALLULLAH.
It was a play.

BILLIE.
Whatever it was,
come and dance with me, lady.

TALLULLAH.
I heard you fell asleep.

BILLIE.
Only when you left the stage, honey.
Only when you left.

TALLULLAH.
Does everyone forgive you once they hear you sing?

BILLIE.
Everybody but me.

TALLULAH.
And what about *your* book?
Will you mention me in yours?

BILLIE.
I'll say you tasted like honey.

TALLULAH.
You'll do no such thing!

BILLIE.
How about a love poem?
Not even a love poem
for my honeysuckle pussy from Allybama.

TALLULAH.
Look at you.
Bloated
and saggy
and those eyes.
You look more exhausted than a hundred and one Hebrew
slaves, Billie.

(Beat.)
You mention me in that book and I'll sue you for every penny
you're worth!
And we all know how desperate you are for a penny these days.

BILLIE.
It's just a book.
I'll write a lot of happy things.
Loving you comes with an aftertaste.
I'll leave that part out.

(The door opens. It's JOE GLASER.)

JOE.
Lady Day's gotta get ready for set number two.

BILLIE.
Fuck you.

JOE.
It's a second set or the poorhouse.
What's it gonna be, Billie?

BILLIE.
Tallulah.
Tell that fat piece of shit I said
Fuck
you.

JOE.
You've got two minutes.
So do whatever it is that you do
and get your ass out on that stage
and sing the fuckin song.

*(He exits. BILLIE grabs a bottle. She drinks. From under a
couch cushion, she begins to prepare a needle.)*

TALLULAH.
That's how you do it, then?
That's how you get out there and sing like that?

That's how you sell it?

BILLIE.
I do this,
that
and the other thing.
And I do them all beautifully.
Just like I did you.
(Beat. She injects herself. A sharp inhale. She speaks the next words on a long, deep exhale.)
But don't worry, Banky.
I won't write about any of those things in my little book.
Not even your honeysuckle secret.

(The door opens again.)

JOE.
Now, Billie.
You wanna get paid tonight,
you'll get out there now.
(Beat. They stand off for a moment, but she finally relents and exits. He turns to TALLULAH.)
The book is going to be about Lady Day.
About her career.
What's to worry about?

TALLULAH.
You were listening.

JOE.
I'm her manager, Miss Bankhead.
I'm always listening.

TALLULAH.
As if she'll write the book herself!
Who's fooling who here, Mr. Glaser?
You'll stick the bitch in a room with a typist and a bottle of
scotch and all the tar she needs for those hungry little veins and
as the time ticks by she'll run her mouth around the moon and
back and my moon, Mr. Glaser,
is not one I wish to read about in a *book*.

(Blackout.)

First Interlude

(An invisible band plays "What A Little Moonlight Can Do" as BILLIE stumbles in and turns on the light. She catches her reflection in the mirror. And someone else's too.)

BILLIE.
Mama.

SADIE.
Did you like it when he climbed on top of you?

BILLIE.
Go away...

SADIE.
You like it when that sleazy nigger climbed up on top of you?
Inside you?
Wilbur Rich.

BILLIE.
You not here, go *away*!

SADIE.
Wilbur fuckin' Rich from just next door!
He was supposed to be watchin' you.
Protectin' you.
Keepin you *safe*.
And Mama, well she just left you for a little while.
Left you there with your scrambled eggs and bacon.

BILLIE.
Breakfast for dinner...

SADIE.
You loved that.

(BILLIE frantically dials the phone. We can hear it ringing in

her ear, then a voice on the other line, inaudible.)

BILLIE.
Hello,
yes, hello--

SADIE.
You loved breakfast for dinner, remember, baby?

BILLIE.
I'm calling--
I'm calling to see if there's someone--
If someone is staying at your hotel--

SADIE.
And Bessie was on the radio
cause you--
You loved your Bessie Smith, baby!

BILLIE.
I'm a friend.

SADIE.
Bacon
and eggs
and Bessie
and Wilbur Rich
and now look what baby's turned into...

BILLIE.
An old friend.

SADIE.
A five dollar whore that can barely croak out the blues.

(SADIE disappears, but BILLIE doesn't notice.)

BILLIE.
I'm looking for a Tallulah.
Tallulah Bankhead.
Got more than one Tallulah in your establishment?

(Beat.)
Yes, the actress.
(Beat.)
I'm not a fan, I'm--
This is Billie Holiday!
Lady BillieFuckingHoli Day!
(Beat.)
Alright.
I'll try another.
(Beat.)
Thank you.
(She hangs up and turns around.)
Mama...
(Beat.)
She not here, Billie...
She not here.

Scene 3

(A table in a different club, several months later. It's very late, or very early, depending on how you want to look at it. BILLIE is at a table, chain-smoking and drinking, with LAURA "BIG RED LIVINGSTONE". She is a dancer. Bi-racial. This woman is stylish, sexy and thick in all the right places but she has never had Billie's star quality.)

BILLIE.
(To no one in particular,) I wanted it ten minutes ago.
Asked for the goddamn drink ten minutes ago
and I'm still waiting.
Sang nineteen fucking songs and a lady can't even got a
goddamn drink when she walks off the stage.

BIG RED.
It's coming.

BILLIE.
Don't tell me it's coming.
Christmas is coming.
These drinks are in Timbukfuckintu.

BIG RED.
Who was that?
In the sunglasses before,
who was that?

BILLIE.
A big fat nobody.

(JOE GLASER walks up to the table and tosses ten dollars on the table.)

BILLIE.
What's that?

JOE GLASER.
Your pay.

BILLIE.
That's ten dollars.

JOE.
I'm still payin off that bail money,
ain't I?

BILLIE.
What'm I supposed to do with ten dollars?

JOE.
Use your imagination.

BILLIE.
Cocksucker.

JOE.
The bar cut you off two drinks ago.
Go back to the hotel.

BILLIE.
It's a shithole.
And cut who off?
Cut me off?

Two sets for a bunch of Gershwin loving whities and they're
cutting me off?
Get me another whiskey.

JOE.
They cut you off two drinks ago, Billie.
Don't cause a scene.
You only got two nights left.
Just two.
Don't cause a scene.

BILLIE.
Two more nights for what?
Ten dollars?

JOE.
Twenty if you put 'em together.

BILLIE.
I won't sing.

JOE.
You'll sing.

BILLIE.
Cut me off and I won't sing.

JOE.
I'm going back to the hotel, Billie.
I suggest you do the same.

(He's gone before she can finish speaking.)

BILLIE.
Cocksucking Jew Fuck!

BIG RED.
Come on, now...
You're real tight tonight.

BILLIE.

He's a piece of shit.

BIG RED.
He did you a favor.

BILLIE.
Yeah, right, all I ever hear.

BIG RED.
Who woulda been there?
Me?
I wasn't bailing you out again.
Not me, Billie.
Go back to the hotel.
C'mon.
I'll take you back.

BILLIE.
I'm not in the mood tonight.

BIG RED.
You're gonna drink yourself to death,
you know that?
Gonna drink your ass
and smoke your ass
straight on til death.

BILLIE.
Allright fine,
c'mon,
I'll give you a little taste.

BIG RED.
I don't want you.
Not like this.
Who'd want this?
Call Kay.
Call up Kay and have him come over to the hotel and fuck the
bitch right out of you, Billie,
cause at the rate you're goin'
nobody's comin to see your casket off.

(RED rises.)

BILLIE.
It's a lot.
Y'know?
All this
sometimes
it's
a lot.
Not everything smells like gardenias, baby.
(Beat.)
One time I got up there
went out there cold
went out there me.
And a girl just wants to sing but it's more than that they want.
They want all of you.

BIG RED.
You say that like I don't know.
Like I ain't ever been out there.

BILLIE.
Oh, you been out there, sure...
But never like me.
Never with those dollars comin' up into the sky,
comin' up like you're a five dollar whore that can croak out the
blues.
Oh, you ain't never been out there with a gardenia
when they want you cheap as a dandelion.
But the blues have to pay the bills, baby, so you do what you
gotta do to get out there
to get up there
to be their little black girl
singing those little black songs
takin their cheap ass dollar bills
and givin them all to Joe Cocksucker Jew Fuck Glaser.
(Beat.)
You ain't never been out there like that,
Laura *Big Red* Livingstone.
So when some uppity white bitch from Allybama that I tasted a

couple of times one hot summer blows in after 8, 10, 15, 20
years lookin sweet as a vanilla wafer that would melt in my
mouth and tells me she didn't come to talk in the dark,
I get a little thrown.
I drink a little drink.
I do a little bit of what I do so's that I can get out there and sing
the same goddamn songs all over again.
(Beat.)
It's called survival, baby.

BIG RED.
Find your own way home, Billie.

(BIG RED exits as...)

Second Interlude

*(...BILLIE rises and walks to a payphone. She deposits a coin
and waits. We can hear the phone ringing through the receiver.)*

BILLIE.
This is,
hello,
this is Billie Holiday.
Yes.
Yes, the singer.
Yes, I'm looking--
I'm looking for a friend.
She might be staying--
She could be staying at your hotel.
(Beat.)
Tallulah Bankhead.
Yes.
Yes, the actress.
(Beat.)
You think I got time for jokes?

(She hangs up. Blackout.)

Scene 4

(TALLULAH is pacing in her dressing room, a cigarette in one hand, a drink in the other. DOROTHY PARKER sits in a chair, her back to us.)

TALLULAH.
Sure, it's just one line, Mrs. Parker.
One line in what?
In thirty years?
But I don't forget lines.
Tallulah Bankhead does not forget her lines.

DOROTHY.
Even you forget things, darling.

TALLULAH.
I forget appointments because I'm hungover.
I forget phone numbers because I can't be bothered.
I don't forget my lines.

DOROTHY.
I'm sure no one even noticed.

TALLULAH.
Three hundred people,
I'm sure someone noticed me umming and uhhing my way
through a speech about I don't even remember what.
And if it happens again,
tonight,
Christ,
if it happens again--

DOROTHY.
You'll live.

TALLULAH.
I'll die.

I will DIE, Dorothy.

DOROTHY.
Before you do,
could I *please* get another gin and tonic?

TALLULAH
I was standing there just about to start...
Just about to chew that first syllable--

DOROTHY.
You always do that.

TALLULAH.
It's my signature.
(Beat.)
There I was and there
she
was.

DOROTHY.
Who?

TALLULAH
The bitch!
God forgive me for saying a thing like this
cause you know,
oh, Mrs. Parker, you know I'd never mean it,
but that nigger bitch is sleeping through my favorite part.
Billie fucking Holiday was too tired to see my play.
Billie fucking Holiday couldn't even tell you what my play was
about.
You know, I'd heard--
I'd heard she'd lost it.
The touch.
I'd heard she wasn't anything more than a five dollar whore these
days.
But I wasn't prepared.
Oh, I wasn't prepared to see all those years on her face.

DOROTHY.

She's still a baby!

TALLULAH.
Not when you look at her,
she's not.

DOROTHY.
What? 35?
40, maybe?

TALLULAH.
41.
Just turned.
But you wouldn't know it from looking at her.
All these lines,
skin cracking like the Sahara,
and she's thick,
Dottie.
She's thick and slow
like molasses,
all bloated like.
And her eyes,
lookin everywhere but at you.
Lookin past you and above you and below you and through you
but never at you
cause there's so much else to see when you're high as a Boeing
over Utah.
(Beat.)
I could still taste her though.

DOROTHY.
Careful, Banky...
Even walls have ears.

TALLULAH.
Let them hear me.
What'll happen?
Let them hear me.
She's a *woman*, Mrs. Parker!
A real, live, flesh-eating, fire-breathing woman.
And I can't get the fucking aftertaste out of my mouth.

DOROTHY.
And what are *you*?
When you look in the mirror every morning,
noon
and night,
what are you?

TALLULAH.
I loved her.

DOROTHY.
There's been others, though.

TALLULAH.
None that ever tasted quite as sweet.

DOROTHY.
There will be more.

TALLULAH.
There I am and I can't remember a single line.
But I can remember what she tasted like.
I pretended that she tasted like chocolate.
I would nibble at her fingers and her toes and her thighs and her
tits like they were the ears of a milk chocolate Easter rabbit.
(Beat.)
Pretending wasn't hard.
Not because I'm an actress.
Acting was harder.
Pretending wasn't hard because she tasted like everything:
like chocolate and vanilla and strawberry and apricot and honey
and cinnamon...
And sometimes she'd taste like vinegar, you know, after one too
many? And sometimes--
Sometimes like salty Sunday grits after getting off the stage
but almost *always* like chocolate
because chocolate is my favorite and even when she wasn't Billie
she was always Billie and Billie was my favorite.
(Beat.)

Sometimes I wonder if I was embarrassed about
LOVING her
or
loving HER.
Know what I mean,
Mrs. Green?

DOROTHY.
Did she love you just the same, Tallulah?
(Beat.)
It's a simple yes
or a simple no
and nothing in between.

TALLULAH.
I suppose you'd have to ask her, Mrs. Parker.

DOROTHY.
You'll go mad if you keep wondering.

TALLULAH.
I won't be the first woman to go mad over a lost love.
And I most certainly won't be the last.

DOROTHY.
A couple of pages in a book won't kill you.

TALLULAH.
No, but they'll sting.

DOROTHY.
And you'll deny them the very next day.
Who'd believe her anyway?
Drunk as a skunk on a Tuesday morning,
who'd believe her?

TALLULAH.
I would!
'cause she'd be right.
Tallulah Bankhead won't ever forget the way Billie Holiday
tasted that summer cause Tallulah Bankhead is too busy

forgetting everything else.
(Blackout.)

Third Interlude

(BILLIE stands at a payphone.)

BILLIE.
This is Billie Holiday.
(Beat.)
Yes,
the singer.

(SADIE appears from behind the phone.)

SADIE.
Need a room?

BILLIE.
Go away.
(Into phone,)
No, not you, I'm sorry, I'm just--
just looking for a friend.

SADIE.
Who you lookin' for, baby?

BILLIE.
Thought she might be stayin' there,
at your establishment.

SADIE.
What you lookin' for?

BILLIE.
Tallulah Bankhead?
(Beat.)
Yes,
the actress.

SADIE.
Can't have a bed without a room,

and can't get your way without a bed.

BILLIE.
I know you can't say,
sir,
but--
but everyone else just said no.
Everyone else just said she wasn't there.
So,
if
if you could--
Could you tell her that I--
that Billie Holiday called?
(Beat.)
Yes,
the singer.

SADIE.
If you can't *get* your way
how you gonna *make* your way?

(SADIE exits.)

BILLIE.
Tell her I'll be waiting in the lobby of the Carlton
at seven thirty next Tuesday night.
(Beat.)
And tell her I'll wait as long as I can.

(Blackout.)

Scene 5

(An office filled to the brim with vinyls, posters, press clippings, cigar ash, empty bottles, dirty ashtrays and twenty-five unfinished projects. JOE GLASER sits behind a desk. BIG RED stands across from it. LOUIS MCKAY sits in an armchair nearby. He's a big man. African American. Solid. Terrifying when he needs to be.)

LOUIS MCKAY.

Billie's Billie, baby.
She ain't never gonna stop bein' Billie til she's dead.

BIG RED.
That's just what I'm worried about.

LOUIS.
Me and Mr. Glaser take good care of Billie.
I give her what she needs to give Mr. Glaser what he needs.
And that little merry-go-round keeps goin round and everybody's happy.

BIG RED.
Everybody but Billie.

JOE.
Bullshit.

BIG RED.
You think she likes getting up there?

JOE.
It's what she wanted.
Wasn't it?
Started singing for a reason,
didn't she?

LOUIS.
She's a lady, Red.
She's not a canary.

BIG RED.
It's like this:
Billie used to sing because she had no other way to get all that anger out.
Now
Billie sings cause she's got no other way to live.
It's become her burden.

JOE.
It's a gift.

BIG RED.
Not when the only thing it gives you is misery.
That ain't no gift, Mr. Glaser.

LOUIS.
I don't mean to insult your feelings, Laura--
that is your *real* name,
ain't it?

BIG RED.
You know damn well it's my name, Louis.

LOUIS.
I don't mean to be rude,
Laura,
but I'm a busy man.
I don't have time to beat around your bush.
Who are you to tell us what Billie needs?
That's what she's got me for.
That's what she's got a man for.

JOE.
And an agent, too.

BIG RED.
I'm an old friend.
I know a lot.
I seen a lot.
(Beat.)
You don't know the half of Lady.
You think you got that thousand-piece puzzle all figured out but
I could pretty much guarantee you that you're missing half those
little jigsaw pieces.
(Beat.)
I never seen Lady so tired.
I never seen Lady so angry.
And Lord knows I have seen that woman rage
but I never seen her like this.
Keep feeding her whatever it is that you're feeding her, Louis,

and she'll be gone before you know it.
Poof.
Into thin air.

(Beat.)

LOUIS.
Ban her from the clubs, Joe.

BIG RED.
What?

LOUIS.
I didn't say anything to you.
(To JOE,) Ban her from the clubs.
Every goddamn place my woman sings even half a fucking song,
ban the bitch.
(To BIG RED,)
Come to the house.
See what happens.
Call the house.
See what happens.
I know what's good for Billie.
Mr. Glaser knows what's good for Billie.
And don't think I didn't smell your perfume on her panties last
month when I was in New York.
I've got it all under control.
(Beat.)
You can disappear now.

(He exits as...)

Fourth Interlude

(...BIG RED walks to the payphone, in pinspot.)

BIG RED.
There were lots of us.
Loves, I mean.
Billie collected us like she collected songs.
But I was her favorite.

Even after the loving was over,
I like to think I was her favorite.
(Beat,)
In every single city there was someone Billie could come home
to
'cause Billie hated sleeping alone.
I remember the first time she took me home.
She suckled on my fingertip a minute in the hallway,
just put it in her mouth while she was fumbling with the keys,
and pulled me inside with her lips once the door was open.
Said I tasted like candy coated peanuts.
Sweet but salty.
Not and.
(Beat.)
That always bothered me.
Not sweet *and* salty.
Sweet *but*...
(Beat.)
They weren't all like me either.
White and black,
light and tan,
male or female or somewhere in between.
You love Billie, Billie loves you.
And Billie had loves everywhere she went.
(Beat. A phone begins to ring.)
She don't need a lot to get by.
Least she didn't back then.
Back then she just needed someone.
(Beat.)
Anyone.

*(She slips a coin into the phone and waits. We can hear it
ringing through the receiver. It rings and rings until, finally...
BILLIE answers, sitting up on a bed somewhere, startled awake
in the middle of the night.)*

BILLIE.
Hello?
(Beat.)
Hello,
who's there?

(Beat.)
Say something,
I can hear you breathing.
(Beat.)
Don't call back here again if you ain't gonna say nothing.

(BILLIE hangs up. LAURA stares at the invisible phone for a moment.)

Scene 6

(The bed becomes an examining table as a nurse enters and the lights burn at full glow.)

NURSE.
If you don't mind my asking--

BILLIE.
Depends.

NURSE.
I've always wondered...

BILLIE.
Yeah?

NURSE.
Why gardenias?

BILLIE.
I was doing a show somewhere,
don't remember,
and I burned my damn hair with a curling tongue just before I
had to get on that stage.
Aaaaannnnnnd
this friend
Carmen
yeah
she was in my dressing room
fixing me up
you know

and she said
Carmen said I oughta put a flower or two right there on that spot
where I burned my hair so's I sent Carmen right downstairs to the
florist and she came back with gardenias.
My blood pressure alright?

NURSE
A little high.

BILLIE
Fuck.
(Beat.)
I like the way they smell, though.
Gardenias.
And next night some man in the audience sent back a box of 'em
just before the show.
Said he was there the night before and just had to come back
again.
And
you know,
my hair was still burnt in that spot
so I've been putting them in my hair ever since.
It's my signature.

NURSE.
Could I...

BILLIE.
What?

NURSE.
Could I get an autograph?
It's for my father.
He's a very big fan.

(BILLIE takes the pad from her and signs an autograph.)

NURSE.
Thank you.
And you're here for...

BILLIE.
A cough.
(The NURSE writes as BILLIE speaks.)
Nasty one.
Hurts like a bitch.
Sometimes I can't catch my breath out there.
Those lights get so hot and they beat down on you real hard but
you just gotta keep on singing no matter how fast your heart
beats.
And my side.
Right here.
(She places her hand near her liver.)
It's a dull ache
all
the
fuckin'
time
like I'm all cramped up and tight inside.
Like somebody's got my stomach wrapped up in their fist.

NURSE.
Have you been drinking?

(Beat.)

BILLIE.
Well, course I have a little somethin' now and then,
who doesn't--

NURSE.
The doctor did *warn* you--

BILLIE.
Yeah, but c'mon--
Line of work I'm in people--
People gotta *drink* now and then.

(Beat.)

NURSE.
The doctor will be in soon.

(The NURSE exits abruptly. Blackout.)

Scene 7

(A hotel lobby. TALLULAH is alone in a chair. She is growing impatient. She checks her watch. After a moment, BILLIE enters. They stare at each other for a moment.)

TALLULAH.
It's rude to invite someone
and show up late.

BILLIE.
The elevator was--

TALLULAH.
Your eyes are bloodshot.
I'm not an idiot.

BILLIE.
Don't do that.
Not here.

TALLULAH.
Where then?

BILLIE.
Come upstairs.
Come up and dance with me.

TALLULAH.
Dance? *(She laughs.)*

BILLIE.
Just come up.
Have a drink.
I'll keep the light on.
(She walks to the elevator.)
One drink won't kill you.

TALLULAH.
It's not me I'm worried about.

(They get into the elevator, the lights changing abruptly to reveal the small and suffocating square. This should be fluid. A sound effect can be used if desired. After a moment,)

BILLIE.
It's the slowest goddamn elevator in America.
There's nothing to be worried about.

TALLULAH.
Look at you.
I want to talk to you.
I want to help.

BILLIE.
Billie don't need anybody's help!
Billie does just fine!

TALLULAH.
Billie don't even know what "fine" *is,* she's so damn high.

BILLIE.
You ever try it?
(No response.)
If you ain't ever tried it,
you don't get to knock it.
(Beat.)
You'll come on up and you'll try it, Loolie.
You'll see.
You'll like it.
I promise the whole world sparkles.
(Beat.)
You'll like the way you disappear inside yourself. Everything goes quiet and numb and for the first half hour you'll forget you have toes and you'll never want it to end but somewhere round 8 o'clock you'll get real thirsty and you'll tell yourself to have a glass of water but by habit pour yourself some whiskey and by eight-thirty-five you'll have forgotten all about your legs cause who needs legs when you haven't got any toes?

(She laughs.)
Try it, Banky.
You'll like it til your lips are cracked and the only thing you can taste is tar.
You'll like it til even Gershwin is too hard to sing.
You'll like it til wears off and some old white fuck from Ally-bama wants that goddamn tune about pennies from heaven and you give up halfway through the second verse cause your lips are dryer than the Sahara.
But for a few hours you'll get your
(separating the syllables carefully,)
com-
pre-
hen-
sion.
(Beat. The elevator door opens. 'Ding'.)
Come in and try it, Banky.
Then you can tell me what I *really* taste like.

TALLULAH.
Let go of the door.
(Beat.)
Stop holding the door and let it close.

BILLIE.
What changed?
Don't you want a chapter in my book?

TALLULAH.
I don't want a goddamn *page*!

BILLIE.
The Great Tallulah Bankhead and her honeysuckle cunt.
Even when I got a little hair between my teeth,
she still tasted like sweet iced tea on a hot August morning.

TALLULAH.
Let go of the door, Billie!

BILLIE.
I told you there ain't nothin to worry about

and there ain't.
I'll keep your milky white ass outta my book
and go to my grave tasting honey pie.
Don't you worry,
Miss Bankhead.
The nigger girl ain't gonna tell a soul.

(She lets the door close. Blackout.)

Scene 8

(Several months later. JOE's office. LOUIS is back in his chair and JOE behind his desk. Unfinished drinks of various states sit on the desk. LOUIS smokes a cigar. BILLIE paces, chain-smoking.)

BILLIE.
Just sit in the chair and sign?

JOE.
That's all you gotta do, baby.

BILLIE.
How many?

JOE.
Two hundred copies.
Maybe three.

BILLIE.
One.

JOE.
One-fifty.

BILLIE.
One.

LOUIS.
One-fifty, baby.

(Beat.)

BILLIE.
One-fifty.

JOE.
Sign a couple of books,
say a couple of nice things.
Hello.
How ya doin'.
You know...
Thanks for coming.
What's your favorite tune?

BILLIE.
Fuck that.

JOE.
Just be cordial.

BILLIE.
Favorite tune?
Fuck that.

JOE.
Pretend like you're interested.

BILLIE.
I'm a singer not an actress.
I sing, I don't pretend.
I pretend like I'm interested and pretty soon they got me singin' a capella
and Billie don't sing a capella.
'specially not for no readers.
(Beat.)
Favorite tune.
Fuck that.
Tell 'em to come to the club and I'll sing "A Little Moonlight..."

JOE.
So ask them something else.

BILLIE.
Favorite
fucking
tune--

JOE.
Who's your favorite singer?

BILLIE.
Me.

JOE.
Who's your favorite trumpet player?

BILLIE.
Louis Motherfucking Armstrong.
Bunch of boring people wantin' a book signed.

JOE.
It's *your* book, Billie!

BILLIE.
And it's 100 percent
bull
shit.
They don't wanna hear what *really* happened.
They don't wanna know bout me or The Duchess or Wilbur or a
One Hundred and Fortieth street,

LOUIS.
Not all of it.

BILLIE.
Nah, baby, not all of it,
but just about every little bit.

JOE.
What you gonna do?
What else you gonna say?

Huh?
You go out there,
you sing your songs,
you drink your booze,
you shoot those pretty little chocolate arms full of whatever it
takes to make you Lady fucking Day
and all you do is gripe.
(Beat.)
So, you and your momma slapped a couple of dicks around for a
few extra dollars...
But now look!
(Beat.)
They might be boring.
They might think every word of that book is true.
They might even be your fans.
Stop griping.
Sing the fucking song.
Drink the fuckin booze.
Shoot up.
Do whatever you gotta do
or get back on the street and start giving it up again.

*(Beat. BILLIE picks up a drink from the desk and throws it in his
face.)*

LOUIS.
Baby--

BILLIE.
Fuck you.
I ain't signin' no goddamn books.

*(She exits, slamming the door behind her. Beat. LOUIS takes out
a handkerchief and gives it to JOE, who wipes his face dry.)*

LOUIS.
She's--

JOE.
High.

LOUIS.
Alright, Joe...

JOE.
Or desperate.
When she's not high,
she's desperate.

LOUIS.
She don't like all the lights.
Y'know,
all the people.
Sometimes it's too much.

JOE.
It's what she wanted.
She told me that's what she wanted.

LOUIS.
Billie don't know what she wants anymore.

JOE.
And you do?
(Beat.)
No disrespect, Kay,
but you stroll in here just when she's cleaning up her act and you
plug her up again with all that--
all that *shit*.
That's why she lost her cabaret card in the first place.
All that dope.
And what for?
Sounds like a cat in heat when she's on that.
That voice goes straight to hell.

LOUIS.
Who told the police were that smack was?
(Beat. No answer.)
Huh?
Somebody told them.
Club manager?
Bassist?

Pianist?
Huh?

JOE.
Nobody knows,
What's that matter now anyway?

LOUIS.
I had a couple drinks once with a friend.
A buddy in New York.
Now, Billie--
Billie's stupid sometimes.
Billie's gullible.
Billie likes people til they cross her but sometimes Billie's too
blind to notice they're crossin'.
(Beat.)
I don't care much about proof,
Mr. Glaser,
cause I don't have time for proofin'.
Sure,
I knew Billie then.
Seen her round.
Sampled the pie once or twice.
We wasn't Louis and Billie then but we was
acquainted.
And somebody tells Louis McKay that Lay-dee Day is in the
slammer?
Good thing I got those contacts,
ain't it now?
Times like that a man needs
contacts.

JOE.
It was a rough couple of months.

LOUIS.
I heard Satchmo had it pretty rough then too.

JOE.
Not so bad...

LOUIS.
Nah?
No Mary Jane in his dressing room?

(Beat.)

JOE.
Yeah.
Yeah, a little marijuana.
But Billie--

LOUIS.
BillieBillieBillie!
(Beat.)
Drugs is drugs,
baby.
Y'know, I heard a little story when I had those drinks with my
friend,
my buddy.
Story went like this:
(Beat.)
A sniveling, bald Jew weasel rolled his fat ass into the precinct
and told them he'd give them a little somethin' if they gave old
Satchmo a break.
And that fat fuck strolls over to wait for good ol' Louie
Armstrong,
and when Satchmo comes out,
off they go.
Few hours later,
the Feds are stormin' Billie's apartment,
the fuckin' Feds.
And these guys are lookin' for somethin' a lot harder than grass.
(Beat.)
Now, don't get me wrong,
Joe.
There's a lot of fat, bald, Jewish, sniveling weasels out there.
I don't know many besides you.
But maybe it was a different one.
Maybe that rat was a different one.

JOE.

She needed help, Kay.

LOUIS.
And who gave her that?

JOE.
I thought they'd--

LOUIS.
What? Thought what?

JOE.
I thought they'd help her.
Get her some proper treatment.
I thought it'd force her to get clean.
For good!

LOUIS.
Well, you thought wrong, baby.

JOE.
I didn't know it was gonna be so bad.
I didn't know they'd lock her up like that.
Take away everything she had--

LOUIS
And that's why you been payin' all the bills.
I get it.
I do.
Guilt's a tough thing to live with, Joe.
But payin' her peanuts to sing two sets?
Taking almost her whole damn pay?

JOE.
Somebody's gotta cover all them legal fees, Kay--

LOUIS.
And who's lookin' out for baby?

(Beat. He begins to rise.)

LOUIS.
She'll sign one hundred and fifty books and sing two songs.
Get a pianist.
I'll take care of her.

JOE.
I think she needs a break, Kay.

LOUIS.
Get her a couple of nights somewhere big, too.
Somewhere fancy.

JOE.
Did you hear what I said, Louis?

LOUIS.
Somewhere a lot of white folk go.
Think you can do that, Mr. Glaser?

JOE.
Look at her!
'member how pretty she used to be?
Now look at her!
She's ugly as sin--

LOUIS.
Careful--

JOE.
She is!

LOUIS.
And you're a fine specimen yourself, Mr. Glaser...

JOE.
Excuse me?

LOUIS
Look at you!
That suit's three years old.
I can tell by the elbows.

And what about your hair?
That's goin'.
Your belly sure ain't, cause that just keep gettin' bigger.
Ain't that what happens when you get old, Mr. Glaser?

JOE.
She's a sad sight.
And that voice ain't what it used to be.
Nobody wants her anymore.

LOUIS.
And who wants you?
Who wants Joseph Glaser?
Those little girls you like to play with?
They want you, Mr. Glaser?
Or are they just doin' what you tell them?
Oh, I know all about 'em...
'member that friend, Joe?
That friend told me all about you and your little girls,
'bout your dirty secrets.
(Beat.)
Guess we all got secrets, baby.
And what about the customers?
Do *they* want you?
(Beat.)
Oh, sure they want Billie.
But do they want you?
They want Satchmo,
but do they want *you*?
Satchmo comes in,
he blow that horn,
and everybody loves it.
People don't pretend to be nice to Satchmo.
They worship him.
People don't pretend to be nice to Billie.
They worship her.
People gotta pretend to be nice to you.
(Beat.)
Oh, she might be ugly.
She might be tired.
But that don't mean they don't want her, Mr. Glaser.

(Beat.)
Somewhere big and fancy.
Carnegie Hall.

JOE.
Carnegie!

LOUIS.
Yeah, Joe.
I like the way that sounds.
Carnegie Hall!

(He exits as JOE follows him out. A letter floats down from the ceiling on a string. TALLULAH enters and retrieves it. She opens it and reads.)

Fifth Interlude

TALLULAH.
"Dear Miss Bankhead:

(BILLIE appears in a spotlight.)

BILLIE.
"I thought I was a friend of yours. That's why there was nothing in my book that was unfriendly to you, unkind or libelous... I tried six times last year to talk to you on the damn phone, and tell you about the book just as a matter of courtesy. But that bitch you have who impersonates you kept telling me to call back and when I did, it was the same deal until I gave up... There's nothing in it to hurt you. If you think so, let's talk about it like I wanted to last year. Straighten up and fly right, Banky! Nobody's trying to drag you."

(Beat.)

TALLULAH.
Bitch.

(Blackout.)

Sixth Interlude

(The light on BILLIE fades as TALLULAH speaks. Over the course of the interlude, each speaker should appear in a pool of light. They are all smoking, except for the NURSE. By the end, the stage should almost appear foggy.)

TALLULAH.
Best known for their fragrant white flowers,
gardenias are heat-loving evergreen shrubs
that have become a gardening symbol in the Southeast.

(BIG RED appears lone in another pool of light, smoking.)

BIG RED.
Another common name is
Cape
Jasmine.

(JOE appears alone in another pool of light, smoking.)

JOE.
The plants grow from 2 to 8 feet tall and wide, depending on the variety.

BIG RED.
Got the call after midnight.

(LOUIS appears alone in another pool of light,.)

LOUIS.
Gardenias require at least an inch of rain
or
equivalent watering each week.

TALLULAH.
Maintain room temperature.

BIG RED.
Metropolitan Hospital.

JOE.
Gardenias do best at about 65 degrees Fahrenheit during the
day--

TALLULAH.
--and 55 degrees at night.

LOUIS.
Got the call after midnight.

(SADIE appears lone in another pool of light, smoking.)

SADIE.
Most gardenias grow into a round shape--

(NURSE appears lone in another pool of light, smoking.)

NURSE.
Metropolitan Hospital.

SADIE.
--with dark green, glossy leaves--

BIG RED.
--and white, fragrant flowers.

JOE.
Got the call after midnight.

TALLULAH.
They bloom from mid-spring into summer.

NURSE.
Metropolitan Hospital.

SADIE.

They rarely see winter.

TALLULAH.
And when they do,
they freeze.

(BILLIE passes through them and the fog, now in a hospital gown.)

JOE.
That's where they brought her.
That's where she'd--

BIG RED.
--shrivel up like--

SADIE.
--strange fruit--

BILLIE.
--on a squeaky mattress in 1926.

(They all watch BILLIE exit... TALLULAH goes as the lights burst to a full glow.)

Scene 9

(A hospital waiting room. Everything is white. It's so white it's unsettling. LOUIS is drinking coffee out of a white cup while sitting in a white chair. JOE is standing nearby, along with the NURSE. This is a long stretch of scene-work that should be fluid and without break. BILLIE'S passages should happen around the other characters, none of whom can see or hear her. It is a gradual "passing on". Time moves quickly here. Minutes turn into days and days into weeks in the blink of an eye.)

JOE.
And when will we be able to see her?

NURSE.
The doctor is assessing everything, sir.

The best thing you can do now is to be patient.
Once we know more--

JOE.
Patient?

NURSE.
Yes, sir.
Once we--

JOE.
Do you know who's in that bed?

NURSE.
Yes, sir, I do.

JOE.
You want me to be patient?

NURSE.
I have several of her records, sir.
As does the doctor.
We'd like to have more.

(Beat.)

JOE.
She was supposed to stop drinking.

NURSE.
And did she?

JOE.
For a little while.
Cirrhosis,
he called it.

(She writes something down.)

NURSE.
Has there been anything else besides the drink?

(Beat. A careful one.)

JOE.
No.

NURSE.
Are you certain?

(Beat.)

JOE.
Yes.

NURSE.
Very well.

(She exits. Instantly,)

JOE.
Not a word.
Not a word from Mister Holiday.
Mister Holiday always had a thousand words
but now he hasn't got any.
Not
a
fucking/
word.

LOUIS. *(Overlapping,)*
It's been a long couple of months, Joe.
Okay?
You don't know.

JOE.
I know.
I see her, I hear her.
I don't know?
I know.

LOUIS.

You try.
You beg and you yell and you maybe one time you hit her but
you try
and you try
and
you
try
but Joe,
sometimes she's better.
Sometimes she's on that shit and she's better.

JOE.
Til she crashes!
Then somebody's gotta pick up all the pieces.

LOUIS.
Like in Humpty Dumpty?

JOE.
She's not a nursery rhyme, Kay.

LOUIS.
Ain't she though?
Billie Holiday
came to say
that this would be the way
poor ol' Lay-dee Day
would take her final stay.
(Beat.)
She packed my bags for me.
They were on the stoop.
She
packed them
for me.

(LOUIS looks up as BIG RED enters. Beat.)

BIG RED.
Is she--

LOUIS.

Dead?
(Beat.)
No.

JOE.
Might as well be, though.
(Beat.)
Red,
hello.

BIG RED.
Joe.
(Beat. To LOUIS,)
I didn't think you'd be here.

LOUIS.
I guess she finally started takin' your calls again..
(Beat.)
Oh, well, it's a separation.
Not a divorce.
I got other places to be
but this one trumps.

BIG RED.
Can I see her?

LOUIS.
No.
Not yet.

(BILLIE appears, unseen by the others.)

BILLIE.
Feelin' all swollen there.

BIG RED.
Where did you--
Kay?

BILLIE.
Tummy swollen.

BIG RED.
Where did you find the coffee?

(He doesn't respond.)

BILLIE.
Eyes swollen.
Lips swollen.

BIG RED.
Is it allright?
If I stay?

LOUIS.
Coffee's down the hall.
Here's a nickle.
Stay all you want.

(He holds out a nickle.)

BILLIE.
Fingers swollen.
Pussy swollen.
Liver all shriveled up like a gardenia in December.

(BIG RED takes the nickle and walks past BILLIE to exit as the lights fade to a pinspot on...)

BILLIE.
He raped me,
Mama said.
December Twenty Fourth.
Pretty little things break real easy.
Learned that one early.
Learned that one when I was ten years old and Wilbur Rich
climbed on top of me and put it inside.
Wilbur Rich.
He had nasty breath and nasty teeth and nasty eyes and when he
kissed you it was like kissing a bloodhound,

all this fat
just
jingling
jangling.
Mama walked in just as he was
/cumming.
Felt like hours til he finished
all that shakin and groanin
but I guess it was only a minute
cause 'fore I knew it,
there they were,
bunch of pigs to take me away.
Mama hollered and fought--
But there I was.
House of the Good Shepherd
black and blue all over cause the nuns loved to see me turn
purple like an eggplant.
A whole goddamn year spent hiding in the closet from Sister
Mary Cuntrag.
(Beat.)
Sometimes it's like that.
Sometimes all them lights,
all them people,
that A-string on the bass.
Sometimes it's like hiding in the closet from a nun with a paddle.
You hope they don't look inside.

*(BIG RED re-enters. BILLIE remains, still unseen by the others.
Maybe she sits in the waiting room. Maybe. RED is carrying a
cup of coffee. She sits down and stares at the cup.)*

LOUIS.
You like your coffee, Laura.

BILLIE.
If they look inside the closet--

BIG RED.
I don't like it,
I need it.

BILLIE.
--if they look inside you
they'll find it:

LOUIS.
Seen you drink five, six cups a day all this week.

BILLIE.
All that--
Ugly.

(The light on BILLIE fades as she exits.)

LOUIS.
That's a lot of coffee.

BIG RED.
I think Brazil can keep up.

JOE.
You two talkin' about coffee,
she's in there handcuffed.

BIG RED.
Don't--

JOE.
She can't walk a step,
shittin' all over herself like a baby,
eyes so bloodshot I doubt she can see a goddamn thing
and they've got her there
handcuffed
handfuckingcuffed to the bed!

BIG RED.
She don't know, though!
I hate sayin' it but
Thank God,
Thank God she don't know!
How she gonna?
She don't even know that's me standing over her.

She looked right at me,
you saw her,
looked right at me and called me
Banky.
Who's Banky?

JOE.
Bankhead.
Tallulah Bankhead.
(Beat. A careful one.)
They were--
friends.

BIG RED.
Tallulah Bankhead?
20 years friends she thinks I'm some white bitch from the picture
shows?
That ain't normal.
(Beat.)
She ain't herself.
She ain't Billie.

LOUIS.
Not everybody's themselves when they're dying,
Laura.
That's a fact of life.

BIG RED.
One I'm sure you know all too well.

(Beat.)

LOUIS.
How'd you know who Banky was, Joe?

JOE.
Old stories.
(Beat.)
It was a long time ago.

LOUIS.

You know who Wilbur is?

JOE.
No.

LOUIS.
She kept callin' me Wilbur.
You hear her?

JOE.
Yes, but I--

LOUIS.
That her daddy?

JOE.
I don't know,
Mr. McKay.

LOUIS.
Funny you know Banky, though.

JOE.
Banky and Lady were--
close.

LOUIS.
How close?

JOE.
Close as two people can be.
Like pages in a book
and all those threads in your suit.
Close.

LOUIS.
Did you like to watch?
(Beat.)
Call her up.
Billie wants her old friend Banky?
Call her up.

JOE.
I don't think that's such a good idea--

LOUIS.
Aw, Joey.
Why not?

JOE.
They ain't the best old stories in the world,
Mr. McKay.
Billie broke a lot of vases back then.

LOUIS.
She's not gonna be breakin' any bottles now.
(Beat. Reaching into his pocket for a nickle,)
Call her up.
Walk to that payphone ever,
pop in this nickle and
(He holds it out between his fingers)
call
her
up.

(A long moment passes. JOE eventually takes the coin and begins to go. BIG RED's voice makes him stop.)

BIG RED.
Bille told me once, uh...
She'd been raped.
While she was real little.
Said it was the man from next door.
He was supposed to be watchin' her.
(Beat.)
Said his name was Wilbur.

(Beat.)

LOUIS.
Guess you better call ol' Wilbur up, too, Joe.

Need another nickel?

(Beat. JOE exits. BILLIE enters into a pinspot, followed by NURSE, preparing a needle.)

BILLIE.
Can't I get a little somethin?
Can't you shoot me a little somethin?
Right up this arm'll do.
That'll do right fine.
Gimme a little of that juice and I'll be back to normal.
Would you--
would you believe they took it all?
Just got paid for a couple of sets, too.
Brand new stuff
and they took it all.
All's I got left is seventy cents in a bank account under a name I
destroyed ten years ago.
(Beat.)
Last time they wanted me,
last time they wanted more of me,
I was piss-ass drunk
like the fool from some minstrel show
with powder still on my nose
and a wilting gardenia in my hair.

(A light begins to rise on BIG RED and LOUIS.)

BIG RED.
How many days is it now?

BILLIE.
Ain't never gotta lay on a squeaky mattress when you're singin'.

BIG RED.
Twenty three?

LOUIS.
Twenty *six*.

BIG RED.

Feels like fifty.

LOUIS.
She's a fighter, Billie.
Always has been.

BIG RED.
What do you know about always?
(Beat.)
I'm sorry.
Kay,
I'm--

LOUIS.
You got these big ideas about me, Laura.
That I'm just here to lick the cream off the top.
cagin' Billie up like she's some kinda bird,
that I'm some kinda slave driver
but, baby,
I'm a sharecropper just like you.
Just like Joe.
We're all here to be a part of *her* life.
We're all here for Billie and
Billie...
well...
Billie ain't ever here for us.
Oh, sure, she thinks she is.
She *says* she is...
But Billie can't even be there for herself.
And that's why she's got us wrapped around her fingers.
(Beat.)
What we gonna do when she's gone?
(Beat.)
It's, uh...
S'gonna be another couple days, I think.
'fore she...
(Beat.)
I'm hoping they--
they postpone the arraignment.

BIG RED.

Every time I go in he looks at me cross-eyed.

LOUIS.
All pigs are cross-eyed.
It's a fact.

BIG RED.
Stands there watchin' us like a hawk.
Like I'm gonna help her out the window.
Meanwhile she's dyin' in that bed!

LOUIS.
He ain't goin' nowhere.
Better get used to it cause
long as she's in that room,
he ain't goin' nowhere.

BIG RED.
Who taught her that?
Who taught her to stash it all like that,
stashin' it inside herself like that?

LOUIS.
Nobody taught Billie that, Laura.
Desperation did.
(Beat.)
Let's get some coffee.
Gonna be another long night.

(They exit. JOE enters to the payphone as the lights dim around him. He inserts the coin and dials. It begins to ring. After a few moments, TALLULAH enters. She answers a rotary phone that hangs from another wall of the stage. As he speaks, BILLIE might linger nearby eavesdropping, still unseen.)

JOE.
Tallulah, it's Joe.
Don't hang up,
please don't hang up.
(Beat.)
It's Joe Glaser,

Lady Day's right hand yes man.
Don't hang up, Miss B,
please.
(Beat.)
You don't have to say a word if you don't want,
you've just gotta listen and breathe into the phone every now and
then so I know you're still there.
(She breathes.)
That's real good.
(Beat.)
Lady's not feeling so hot.
Well,
to tell the truth,
she isn't even really herself.
Hardly recognized her when I walked into the hospital room.
All bloated and tiny at the same time.
The emphysema's gotten real bad and her breathing ain't what it
was
and those eyes Satchmo loves are lookin emptier than Lady's
purse.
That poor old tired liver that just can't take no more.
And there's the smack she loves so much...
(Beat.)
Breathe for me, Miss B?
(She does.)
'atta, girl.
(Beat.)
You know they found a secret stash of that shit when they first
brought her in.
Had to cuff her right to the bed.
You believe that?
Cuffing Lady Day to her death bed like she's some common
nigger from the other side of Mississippi.
All cause they found a little smack stashed up inside of her...
(Beat.)
And y'know what I said,
Miss B,
I said its hard being that lady,
or maybe
maybe I said it ain't easy
but whatever it was I said I knew it wasn't--

knew it wasn't right excusing a sight like that.
But what was I gonna do?
I had to protect her,
had to make them *see* that we can't let Lady go out that way,
all chained up to a ghastly little bed at the corner of Life and
Death.
Breathe again for me, Miss.
Let me know you're still there.
(She does.)
Last night we thought we'd lose her between the sickness and the
cravings,
cause she is itchin for a fix and the hospital sure ain't giving her a
taste of tar,
but Lady's tough as nails and refuses to go
and this morning...
This morning she was askin' for you.
Calling your name...
(Beat.)
Think she wants say goodbye.
Can you do that for me, Miss B?
Can you do that,
Tallulah?

*(BILLIE is gone. A long beat. TALLULAH hangs up the phone
and exits.)*

JOE.
Hello?
(Beat.)
If you're still there, breathe for me.
Please, breathe for me...

*(He waits a moment, then finally hangs up the phone. The lights
change as the receiver hits its cradle. LOUIS and BIG RED are
standing, waiting for him to tell them what's happened. JOE
takes a moment before turning around to face them.)*

LOUIS.
Well, then, captain?

JOE.

No go,
Mr. McKay.

LOUIS.
The lady doth protest too much.

BIG RED.
Shakespeare?

LOUIS.
I am not uncultured.
Banky must not love Billie all that much.

BIG RED.
Or maybe--
too much?

(Beat.)

LOUIS.
What do we once she's gone?

BIG RED.
Don't.

LOUIS.
Somebody has to.

BIG RED.
Can't we worry about it when it comes?

LOUIS.
It's comin', honey.
Death ain't takin' no holiday anytime soon.
Time to wake up,
can't throw no ordinary funeral.
Not for Lady Day, no ma'am.

JOE.
I'll take care of it.

LOUIS.
It should be the husband's job--

BIG RED.
Husband?

LOUIS.
Yes.

BIG RED.
You haven't been a husband to her in months--

JOE.
I
will take care of it.
(Beat.)
No, disrespect, Mr. McKay.
But I gotta do this.

LOUIS.
We all got things to be sorry about, Joe.
People to be sorry for.

JOE.
I think--
I think it's the right thing to do.
For Lady.

LOUIS.
Allright then.

(Beat. The NURSE enters, unnoticed.)

NURSE.
Excuse me--

LOUIS.
/Yeah?

JOE. *(Overlapping,)*
What is it?

NURSE.
You'll want to come now.

JOE.
Is she still handcuffed to that bed?

(NURSE nods.)

LOUIS.
Jesus /Christ--

JOE. *(Overlapping,)*
No.
No, I can't look /at that.

BIG RED. *(Overlapping,)*
Won't they--
won't they take 'em off?

NURSE.
No.

BIG RED.
Not even now?

NURSE.
I'm /sorry.

LOUIS. *(Overlapping,)*
(Under his breath,) Mothafuckers.

(LOUIS and BIG RED begin to follow the NURSE out. JOE hesitates.)

BIG RED.
Aren't you coming?

JOE.
Go on without me.

Don't think...
Don't think I'm ready.

LOUIS.
What's the matter, Joe?
Too scared to look her in the eye one last time?

(Beat. No response. LOUIS exits. BIG RED waits.)

BIG RED.
We all tried to save her, Joe.

LOUIS.
Yeah, but what if I tried *too* hard, Red?

(He looks at her. A moment passes.)

NURSE.
Miss?

BIG RED.
Yeah.
(Beat.)
Yeah allright, let's go.

(They exit. The lights fade around JOE. He is alone in pinspot.)

JOE.
I stayed in the waiting room on July 17th.
And when Red came to tell the news,
I went back over to the payphone and ordered five hundred
gardenias.
I'll never forget the smell of them all throughout the services.
The service was, uh...
It was modest.
There wasn't a lot of money.
Seventy cents, to be precise.
Billie had seventy cents in her bank account.
(Beat.)
A few days after she was buried,
a check arrived in the mail.

(A letter falls from the sky and into his lap. He reads...)

"Dear Jonas: This is one letter it is a pleasure for me to write, even with Billie gone just two weeks today. You will find enclosed a check made payable to Billie Holiday from MGM Records in the amount of $1200 on a deal made by Bert Block in this office about three months ago. I really and truly have $120 commission coming on this check however I would advise you to deposit it to Lady's estate. Sincerely yours, Joe Glaser."

I couldn't keep takin'.
No.
Not from Lady Day.
Not anymore.

(The light fades on him as a pool appears over TALLULAH. She stands in a nightgown, with her fur coat over it.)

Seventh Interlude

TALLULAH.
I got in a cab and I went to the hospital.
I already knew where she'd be:
Metropolitan Hospital.
'course I knew.
It was in the papers every day.
Oh, sure the page numbers got higher as the weeks went on but there it was in ink every goddamn day taunting me like her legs.
"Billie Holiday Handcuffed To Death Bed"
"Lady Day Counting Her Days"
"Drugs And Booze Spell Lady Day's Demise"
(Beat.)
Vultures.
That's all they've ever been,
the bastards.
Vultures!
(She spits.
Beat.)
The cabbie was quick.
Efficient.

A little too hospitable for my tastes that evening,
but c'est la vie.
(Beat.)
His name was Jim.
Jim and I chatted as the meter ticked on...
Quite a while, really.
Felt like an hour, but maybe it was half
when I finally told him I wouldn't be getting out.
That I wouldn't be going inside.
That he could drive me home.
(Beat.)
I wanted to remember one hot summer morning in August when
we both woke up early to find a poor fat pigeon on the open
window sill.
We watched him for a while,
Billie and I,
until he finally felt our eyes and flew off startled.
We'd slept naked the night before.
It wasn't just those hot summer nights, either.
Oh, no.
We slept like that every night,
skin
to
skin.
And after that poor fat pigeon flew off,
we made love for hours.
Maybe even days.
And she tasted like hot chocolate and marshmallows on a snowy
winter's night.
While sitting in front of the fire!
(Beat.)
Fourteen dollars on a goddamn taxi-cab I never even got out of.
(Beat.)
I should've put her in my book.
Maybe she would've put me in hers.
After all...

*(BILLIE enters. She and TALLULAH look at each other for a
moment.)*

TALLULAH.

That's what we both wanted in the end.
Isn't it?

(BILLIE runs on, childlike, SADIE close behind, with a plate of breakfast. TALLULAH observes their interaction.)

SADIE. Breakfast for dinner, baby, breakfast for dinner.

BILLIE. Oh, boy, oh, boy--

SADIE. I know it's your favorite.

BILLIE. It is, mama!

SADIE. So, you'll understand I gotta go out.
For a little bit, Just a little bit.
And Mr. Rich, he's gonna--

BILLIE. *(Overlapping,)*
From next door?

SADIE. Yeah, baby,
Mr. Rich is gonna come and watch you while I'm gone.

BILLIE.
He looks at me funny.

SADIE.
What's that supposed to mean?

BILLIE.
I don't know, he just--
He looks at me funny.

SADIE.
Mama's gotta work, Eleanora.
What you want from me?
(Beat.)
Eat your eggs.
You be nice to Wilbur, allright?

BILLIE.
Allright...

SADIE.
Mama see you later...

(She kisses her daughter's head as BILLIE pushes her eggs around the plate. She removes her apron, places it on the back of the chair and exits. BILLIE watches her go. TALLULAH steps into BILLIE's line of vision and smiles.)

BILLIE.
I just keep waitin'...

TALLULAH.
For what?

BILLIE.
I don't know anymore.

TALLULAH.
Come here, Billie.
Come and dance with me.

(BILLIE rises and walks to TALLULAH. They dance for a few moments.)

BILLIE.
This ain't real.
You ain't here.

TALLULAH.
No.
I'm outside in a cab.
Too scared to come in and see you.
(Beat.)
I should've come and held you.
Bathed you.
Oiled your hair with my tears.
Given ya a little rouge.
Made ya feel good before you...

Before....
(Beat.)
Billie.
Billie, Billie, Billie.

BILLIE.
It's time,
ain't it?

TALLULAH.
My cab is leaving.

BILLIE.
So's mine, Banky.

*(TALLULAH stops the dance and walks behind BILLIE. She
unzips her dress and lets it fall. BILLIE stands in a slip. The
other characters enter one at a time, each adding a piece of
BILLIE's wardrobe. SADIE should be last. This process should
take some time. By the end, BILLIE is in an evening gown. There
are pearls around her neck. Long black gloves on each hand.
She is glowing. The happiest we've ever seen her. No gardenia,
though.... Not just yet.)*

BILLIE.
Three things you need out there to make the people happy...
One:
Your hair done up real nice with a gardenia.
Two:
A little juice in your arm.
And
Three:
A tune you can hum.
(Beat.)
Know what I thought first time out there?
First time singing on a stage?
All these hands pop into the sky, waving 'round five dollar bills.
Five dollar bills saying
come.
Know what I thought?
Thought about squeaky mattresses and sweaty eyebrows and

nasty breath and bloodhound kisses.
Thought about a-hundred-and-fifty-one west hundred-and-
fortieth street
and Florence Williams
and all the other girls
and those five dollar bills I got for all them bloodhound kisses.
(Beat.)
But now...
(Beat.)
Now they just like my singin'.
(Beat.)
I had a lotta time to think,
layin' there cuffed to that bed.
Lotta time to think about what I'd say when I got there and
Mister was counting up my sins.
How I'd make it up to Him.
Got a lotta ugly in here, I'd say.
But then I guess He'd already know.
Bet He's got a book that write itself whenever I shoot up or tell a
lie or hate my momma or have a drink or cuss.
(Beat.)
Bet that's a real long book.
(Beat.)
Been waitin' a while here.
Been waitin' with momma a while.
Feels like years,
but maybe it's only minutes.
She leaves,
I wait.
She keeps leavin',
I keep waitin'.
What for, I don't know. *(Beat.)*
If it's a light, I hope it's warm.
Maybe a pink one, even.
If it's a bed, I hope it's soft.
And if it's a bar, I hope it's crowded.
You always need people.
The sounds of 'em all:
somebody laughin', clinking silverware, ice cubes meltin',
somebody flirtin', waiters waitin', empty glasses singin', couples
couplin', people peoplin'.

And just before they announce me,
just
before...
There's silence.
A real *eager* silence.
(Beat. She relishes this.)
And then...
It begins.

*(Applause. Cheers, hoots, hollers. It grows and grows until it is
deafening. A gardenia falls from the sky. She catches it, smells it,
smiles at us. The applause is abruptly silenced with a blackout.
END OF PLAY.)*

ACKNOWLEDGMENTS

Writing this play would not have been possible without the assistance of The Louis Armstrong Archive at Queens Library and archivist Ricky D. Riccardi. Additional thanks to Francesca MacAaron and all others who participated in early readings of this play.

Great thanks are due to Georganne Guyan Bender, Charles Busch, Robert Featherstone, Jean Ann Garrish, Barbara Goetz, Irma and Sol Gurman, Julie Halston, James Horan, Lucille Kenney, Rich Kizer, JoAnn Mariano, Patti Mariano, Dale McCausland, Polly McKie, William Shuman, Samantha Mercado-Tudda, Carey Purcell, Vanessa Spica, Celia St. John and The Drama Book Shop for their encouragement.

Overwhelming gratitude to Albert J. Pica, Theresa Pica, Susan Percoco and Steve McCasland for their unwavering support throughout the years.

ABOUT THE AUTHOR

Steven Carl McCasland is the founder and Artistic Director of The Beautiful Soup Theater Collective. A Pace University graduate, Steven's critically acclaimed plays have been seen in New York and Bermuda. In 2009, Steven was commissioned to adapt poet Jack Wiler's anthologies into a solo performance about Wiler's struggle with HIV. That play, *Fun Being Me*, was workshopped with Jack in the title role before his passing in 2009. Steven's other plays include: *When I'm 64, Hope & Glory, Opheliacs Anonymous, Blue, Pulchritudinous,* Huntington Award in Playwriting - First Place), and *Billy Learns About Captain Kirk* have all received productions regionally and in Manhattan. In June of 2011, Steven premiered his original adaptation of Lewis Carroll's *Alice's Adventures in Wonderland*. Setting Wonderland in the heart of Paris, he also directed and was featured in the cast as the Mock Turtle. After its one week workshop, *Alice Au Pays Des Merveilles* was picked up for an extended run at The SoHo Playhouse through September. His acclaimed play *neat & tidy* made a splash on the Bowery in May of 2012, with critics hailing McCasland as a new Thornton Wilder and the play as one of the Top Dramatic Plays of the year. After critically acclaimed workshops of Steven's plays *Little Wars* and *What Was Lost* in 2014, Beautiful Soup partnered with The Clarion Theatre to present five of his plays in repertory. Those five plays began on May 7th, 2015 and ran through the end of the month. Also featured in rep were *28 Marchant Avenue, Der Kanarienvogel (The Canary)* and a revival of *neat & tidy*. His writing has been acclaimed by New York critics as "brilliant", "riveting", "mesmerizing" and "extraordinary".

Made in the USA
Columbia, SC
23 December 2017